Cookbook for Girls

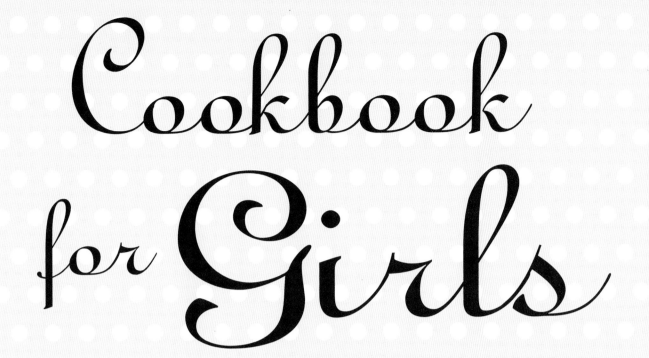

Written by Denise Smart
Photography by Howard Shooter

LONDON, NEW YORK, MUNICH,
MELBOURNE AND DELHI

Project Editor Heather Scott
Senior Designer Lisa Crowe
Home Economist Denise Smart
Craft Designer/Stylist Suzie Harrison
Indexer Julia March
Brand Manager Lisa Lanzarini
Publishing Manager Simon Beecroft
Category Publisher Alex Allan
Print Production Amy Bennett
Production Editor Clare McLean

First published in Great Britain in 2008
by Dorling Kindersley Limited,
80 Strand, London WC2R 0RL
Copyright © 2008 Dorling Kindersley Ltd.
A Penguin Company

8 10 9 7
023 - GD114 – 05/08

ISBN: 978-1-40533-261-3
Reproduced by Alta Image, UK
Printed and bound by Hung Hing, China

Acknowledgements
p119 (t, r) Tim Ridley © Dorling Kindersley;
p121 (t, l), p123 (t, r) and p124 (t) © Dorling
Kindersley; p123 (t, l) Andy Crawford ©
Dorling Kindersley.

The publisher would like to thank the
photographer's assistant Ria Osborne for all
her help, and the following girls for being
fantastic hand models and trainee chefs:
Eleanor Bullock, Hannah Moore,
Elise Flatman and Mykelia Hill.

Discover more at
www.dk.com

Contents

Introduction

This book is all about creating truly scrumptious food that you and your friends and family will love to eat. There are some old favourites as well as new ideas to inspire you to get in the kitchen and start cooking!

Getting started

1 Read the recipe thoroughly before you begin.

2 Wash your hands, tie your hair back (if necessary) and put on your apron.

3 Gather all the ingredients and equipment you need before you begin.

4 Start cooking!

Safe cooking

Cooking is great fun, but with heat and sharp objects around you must always take care to be safe and sensible.

- Use oven gloves when handling hot pans, trays or bowls.
- Don't put hot pans or trays directly onto the work surface – use a heatproof trivet, mat, rack or board.
- When you are stirring food on the cooker, grip the handle firmly to steady the pan.
- When cooking on the stove, turn the pan handles to the side (away from the heat and the front) so that you are less likely to knock them over.
- Take extra care on any step where you see the warning triangle symbol.

Beef chow mein p48

Kitchen hygiene

After safety, cleanliness is the most important thing to be aware of in the kitchen. Here are a few simple hygiene rules for you to follow.

Wash your hands after handling raw meat

- Always wash your hands before you start cooking, and after handling raw meat.
- Wash all fruit and vegetables.
- Use separate chopping boards for meat and vegetables.
- Keep your cooking area clean and have a cloth handy to wipe up any spills.
- Store cooked and raw food separately.
- Always check the use-by date on all ingredients. Do not use them if the date has passed.
- Keep meat and fish in the refrigerator until you need them and always take care to cook them thoroughly.

Always wash fresh fruit and vegetables

How to use the recipes

There's a lot of information packed on each page. Use the key below to find out what each feature tells you, including how long it takes to prepare, cook and how many it serves.

This tells you which section the recipe is from.

Check here for quantity of servings and preparation and cooking times in minutes, unless otherwise stated.

The intro tells you a bit about the dish.

Collect all the ingredients and equipment before you start.

Top tips provide useful suggestions and alternatives.

Step-by-step pictures and text guide you through the recipes.

This sentence gives you helpful hints about when to enjoy each dish.

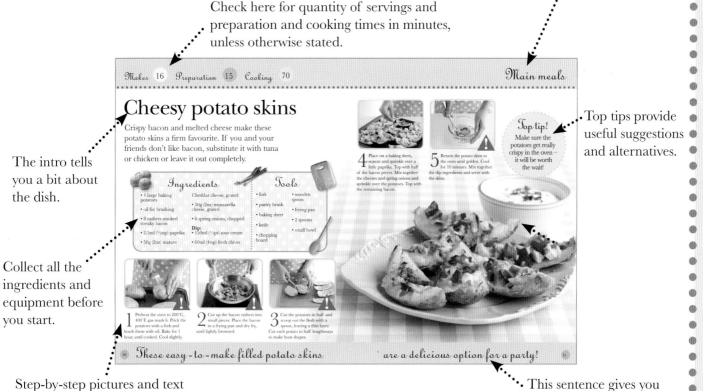

Makes 16   Preparation 15   Cooking 70   Main meals

Cheesy potato skins

Crispy bacon and melted cheese make these potato skins a firm favourite. If you and your friends don't like bacon, substitute it with tuna or chicken or leave it out completely.

Ingredients
- 4 large baking potatoes
- oil for brushing
- 8 rashers smoked streaky bacon
- 2.5ml (½tsp) paprika
- 50g (2oz) mature

Cheddar cheese, grated
- 50g (2oz) mozzarella cheese, grated
- 6 spring onions, chopped

Dip:
- 150ml (¼pt) sour cream
- 60ml (4tsp) fresh chives

Tools
- fork
- pastry brush
- baking sheet
- knife
- chopping board
- wooden spoon
- frying pan
- 2 spoons
- small bowl

Top tip! Make sure the potatoes get really crispy in the oven – it will be worth the wait!

1. Preheat the oven to 200°C, 400°F, gas mark 6. Prick the potatoes with a fork and brush them with oil. Bake for 1 hour, until cooked. Cool slightly.

2. Cut up the bacon rashers into small pieces. Place the bacon in a frying pan and dry fry, until lightly browned.

3. Cut the potatoes in half and scoop out the flesh with a spoon, leaving a thin layer. Cut each potato in half lengthways to make boat shapes.

4. Place on a baking sheet, season and sprinkle over a little paprika. Top with half of the bacon pieces. Mix together the cheeses and spring onions and sprinkle over the potatoes. Top with the remaining bacon.

5. Return the potato skins to the oven until golden. Cool for 10 minutes. Mix together the dip ingredients and serve with the skins.

These easy-to-make filled potato skins   are a delicious option for a party!

Snacks

Red pepper hummous

This roasted red pepper hummous makes a perfect dip for snacking with toasted pitta or crudités. Alternatively, spread onto tortillas with some crumbled feta cheese for an easy wrap.

Ingredients

- 2 red peppers, deseeded and each cut into 4
- 400g (14oz) can chickpeas, drained and rinsed
- 2 cloves garlic, peeled
- 30ml (2tbsp) tahini (sesame seed paste)
- juice ½ lemon
- 45ml (3tbsp) olive oil
- a little paprika

Tools

- knife
- food processor
- plastic bag
- bowl

1 Place the red peppers under a hot grill. Grill until the skins have blackened. Place in a plastic bag and when cool, peel off the blackened skin.

2 Place the skinless peppers with the remaining ingredients in a food processor and blend until smooth and creamy.

3 Transfer the hummous to a bowl and sprinkle with a little paprika. Serve with grilled pitta breads or vegetable crudités.

This healthy snack is great served with

Top tip!

Wait until the peppers are cool before you peel the skin off – you don't want burnt fingers!

vegetable dippers like carrot and cucumber

Griddled fruit & honey

You will love this fruit griddled – it helps bring out the sweetness. If you don't have a griddle pan, place the fruit under a hot grill.

Ingredients

- 3 peaches
- 4 apricots
- 30ml (2tbsp) caster sugar
- 2.5ml (1/2tsp) ground cinnamon
- 200ml (7floz) Greek yogurt
- 30ml (2tbsp) clear honey

Tools

- knife
- chopping board
- 2 mixing bowls
- 2 metal spoons
- griddle pan
- tongs

1 Cut each peach in half and remove the stone. Then cut each into quarters. Halve the apricots and remove the stones.

2 In a large bowl, mix together the sugar and cinnamon, then add the fruit. Toss to coat in the sugar mixture.

3 Preheat a griddle pan and add the peaches, flesh side down. Cook for 2 to 3 minutes. Add the apricots, and turn over the peaches. Cook until caramelised.

4 Meanwhile, place the yogurt in a bowl and pour over the honey. Stir to create a rippled effect. Serve the warmed griddled fruit with the yogurt and honey dip.

Slices of mango and pineapple

Top tip!

If you don't like Greek yogurt, try this with ice cream or crème fraîche.

Cheese & pesto straws

Flavoured with pesto and cheese, these light crisp straws are perfect for dipping.

These moreish cheese & pesto straws

Ingredients

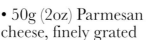

- 200g (7oz) plain flour

- 125g (4½oz) chilled butter, cut into small cubes

- 50g (2oz) Gruyère or Cheddar cheese, finely grated

- 50g (2oz) Parmesan cheese, finely grated

- 1 whole medium egg, plus 1 yolk

- 30ml (2tbsp) pesto sauce (either red or green)

Tools

- sieve
- mixing bowl
- metal spoon
- rolling pin
- knife

- baking paper
- baking sheet
- cooling rack

1 Preheat the oven to 180°C, 350°F, gas mark 4. Sift the flour into a bowl with a pinch of salt. Add the butter and rub in until it looks like fine breadcrumbs.

2 Stir in 75g (3oz) of the cheeses. Beat together the egg and egg yolk and stir into the flour with the pesto sauce. Mix to a dough.

3 The mixture should be of the consistency where you can roll it into a ball.

4 Roll out on a lightly floured surface into a rectangle about 28cm (11in) x 23cm (9in). Cut in half down the longest length, then cut each into about 15 straws.

5 Line a baking sheet with baking paper. Transfer the straws to the baking sheet, leaving a gap between each.

6 Sprinkle over the remaining cheese and chill for 15 minutes. Bake for 12 to 15 minutes. Cool for 5 minutes on the sheet, then transfer to a cooling rack.

are great for parties and picnics

Nachos & salsa

Make this quick tomato salsa and spoon over tortilla chips with cheese for a tasty snack.

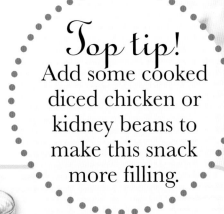

Top tip! Add some cooked diced chicken or kidney beans to make this snack more filling.

Ingredients

- 1 x 200g (7oz) pack plain tortilla chips
- 50g (2oz) mozzarella cheese, grated
- 50g (2oz) mature Cheddar cheese, grated

Salsa:
- 350g (12oz) tomatoes
- ½ red onion, finely chopped
- 2 cloves garlic, crushed
- juice ½ lime
- 60ml (4tbsp) freshly chopped coriander
- 2.5ml (½tsp) sugar
- 1 green chilli, deseeded and chopped

Tools

- chopping board
- knife
- mixing bowl
- metal spoon
- baking tray

1 Cut the tomatoes in half and remove the seeds, then dice. Place in a bowl and stir in all the remaining salsa ingredients.

2 Place the nachos on a large baking tray or shallow ovenproof dish and spoon over the salsa.

3 Scatter over the cheese. Place under a preheated grill for 3 to 4 minutes until the cheese has melted.

Nachos are a tasty Mexican snack made

Top tip!
Serve with sour cream and guacamole to dip your delicious nachos into.

from fried or baked corn tortillas

Spicy potato wedges

These spiced potato wedges can be eaten as a snack, served with a cooling sour cream and chive dip. Alternatively, they make a great accompaniment to the burgers on page 42.

Ingredients

- 3 medium baking potatoes, (about 650g or 1lb 4oz)
- 30ml (2tbsp) olive oil
- 15ml (1tbsp) paprika
- 10ml (2tsp) ground cumin
- 10ml (2tsp) dried mixed herbs
- 2.5ml (½tsp) cayenne pepper (optional)
- 2.5ml (½tsp) salt

Tools

- knife
- chopping board
- large saucepan
- mixing bowl
- metal spoon
- non-stick baking tray
- pastry brush

1 Preheat the oven to 200°C, 400°F, gas mark 6. Cut each potato into 8 wedges.

2 Bring a pan of water to the boil, add the potatoes and simmer for 8 minutes. Drain and return to the pan. Allow to cool slightly.

3 In a bowl, mix together all the remaining ingredients; add the potatoes and toss gently to coat in the spice mixture.

4 Place on a non-stick baking tray, skin side down, and brush with any remaining spice mixture. Cook for 20 to 25 minutes until golden.

These spicy potato wedges are a

Top tip!
Make sure the wedges get nice and crispy in the oven before taking them out.

healthy and delicious alternative to chips

Vegetable tempura

Ingredients

Peanut dipping sauce:
- 15ml (1tbsp) sesame seeds

- 30ml (2tbsp) smooth, unsalted peanut butter

- 15ml (1tbsp) dark soy sauce

- 15ml (1tbsp) rice wine vinegar

- 15ml (1tbsp) cold water

- 10ml (2tsp) caster sugar

- 2.5ml (½tsp) chilli powder

- vegetable oil, for frying

Tempura batter:
- 200g (7oz) self-raising flour

- 5ml (1tsp) cornflour

- 2 egg yolks

- 350ml (12floz) ice-cold water

- 450g (1lb) mixed vegetables

Tools

- frying pan
- measuring jug
- wooden spoon
- chopstick
- 2 bowls
- saucepan
- whisk
- slotted spoon

These vegetables are cooked in a light, crisp batter and served with dipping sauce. Choose a selection of your favourite vegetables.

1 Prepare the dip. Place the sesame seeds in a frying pan and cook over a moderate heat until lightly toasted.

2 Place the sesame seeds in a bowl and whisk in all the remaining dressing ingredients, until well combined and smooth.

3 Place the flours in a bowl. Whisk the egg yolks with the chilled water. Add this to the flour and mix using a chopstick. The mixture should be lumpy.

4 Fill a saucepan ⅓ full of oil and heat to 180°C (350°F). Dip the vegetables in the batter and fry them for 2 to 3 minutes. Remove with a slotted spoon.

These also taste delicious served

Top tip!

Button mushrooms, small cauliflower florets, courgettes, red pepper or carrots cut into thin strips all work well in this recipe.

with sweet chilli dipping sauce

Light meals

Bruschetta

Bruschetta is a tasty Italian starter or snack. It is traditionally made by piling ripe tomatoes onto toasted garlicky bread.

Top tip!
Try adding some torn mozzarella, which can also be lightly toasted under a grill.

Ingredients

- 4 x 2.5cm ($^1/_2$in) slices Italian style bread such as ciabatta
- 3 medium ripe tomatoes
- 15ml (1tbsp) olive oil
- 6 basil leaves
- 1 clove garlic, peeled

Tools

- knife
- chopping board
- metal spoon
- sieve
- bowl
- griddle pan

1 Halve and deseed the tomatoes. Press the seeds through a sieve over a bowl, then discard the seeds. Dice the tomatoes and add to the bowl.

2 Add the olive oil, salt and freshly ground black pepper. Leave to stand for 30 minutes. Roll up the basil leaves, chop finely, then add to the mixture.

3 Toast the bread on both sides, preferably in a griddle pan to create dark lines, or under a preheated grill.

4 Rub the hot bread with the clove of garlic. Place each piece of bread on a plate and heap with the tomato mixture.

Use the freshest ingredients to make

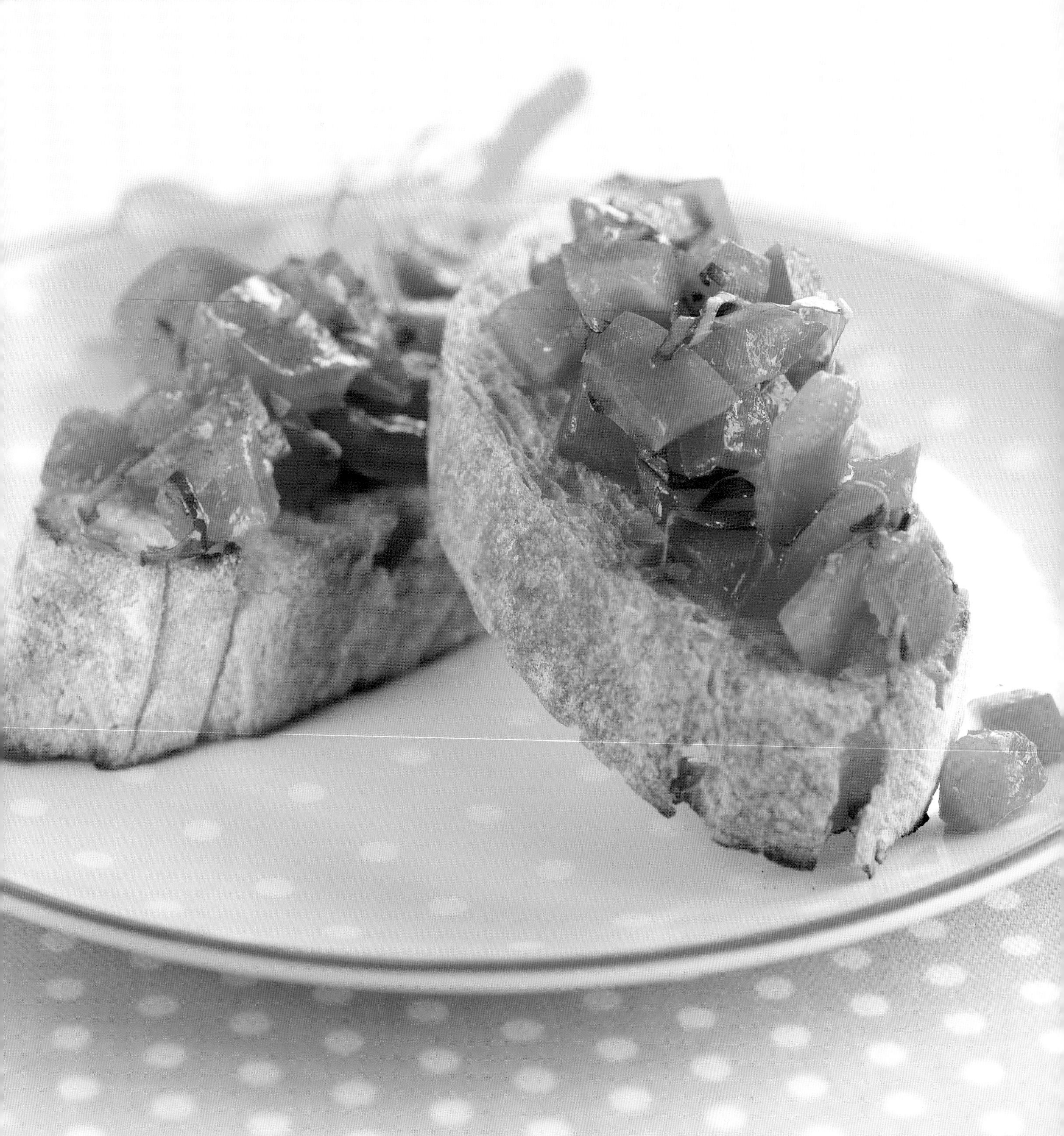

these deliciously simple bruschetta

Jewel salad

This colourful salad made with couscous and pretty pomegranate seeds makes a great accompaniment or a light meal.

Ingredients

- 200g (7oz) couscous

- 300ml (¹/₂pt) hot vegetable stock

- 250g (9oz) cherry tomatoes

- ¹/₂ cucumber

- 1 medium sized pomegranate

- 30ml (2tbsp) olive oil

- grated zest and juice 1 lemon

- 1 small red onion, thinly sliced

- 200g (7oz) feta cheese, crumbled

- large bunch (about 6tbsp) freshly chopped mint

Tools

- 3 bowls
- knife
- measuring jug
- teaspoon
- fork
- wooden spoon
- chopping board

1 Place the couscous in a large bowl and pour over the hot stock and leave for 5 minutes until all the liquid has been absorbed. Allow to cool completely.

2 Cut the cherry tomatoes in half. Halve the cucumber lengthways and scoop out the seeds with a teaspoon, then cut into pieces.

3 Cut the pomegranate in half, and hold one half over a bowl. Lightly tap the pomegranate with a wooden spoon, until the seeds fall into the bowl.

4 Stir the lemon juice, zest and olive oil into the couscous. Add the tomatoes, cucumber, red onion, feta cheese and mint, then stir in the pomegranate seeds.

You can find pomegranates in

Top tip!
You can buy
pomegranate seeds
from the supermarket
if you are in
a hurry!

Club sandwich

This club sandwich is made using ham, chicken and cheese on toasted bread. However, you can use any combination of your favourite meats or cheeses.

This is a super deluxe sandwich —

Ingredients

- 4 slices white bread
- 2 slices wholemeal bread
- 60ml (4tbsp) mayonnaise
- 15ml (1tbsp) lemon juice
- 50g (2oz) shredded iceberg lettuce
- 2 slices Swiss or Cheddar cheese
- 2 slices ham
- 1 tomato, sliced
- 50g (2oz) cooked chicken breast, shredded

Tools

- bread knife
- chopping board
- mixing bowl
- metal spoon
- cocktail sticks

1 Lightly toast the bread on both sides under a preheated moderate grill or in a toaster. Cut off the crusts.

2 In a small bowl mix together the mayonnaise and lemon juice. Season to taste. Stir in the shredded lettuce.

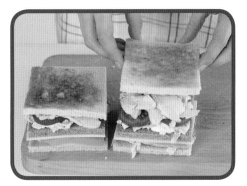

3 Spread 2 slices of the white toast with half of the lettuce and mayonnaise mixture.

4 Place a slice of ham, then a slice of cheese on top of each. Top with the wholemeal bread, spread with the remaining lettuce and mayonnaise.

5 Add some slices of tomato and the chicken. Top with the remaining white toast.

6 Cut each sandwich into 4 triangles and secure each with a cocktail stick.

perfect for a luxurious lunch!

Chicken pasta salad

Ingredients

- 125g (4oz) pasta bows

- 10ml (2tsp) sunflower oil

- 15ml (1tbsp) medium curry paste

- 3 spring onions, chopped

- 1 ripe mango

- juice 1/2 lemon

- 100ml (3 1/2 floz) low fat yogurt

- 100ml (3 1/2 floz) mayonnaise

- 350g (12oz) cooked chicken breast, diced

- 30ml (2tbsp) freshly chopped coriander

- 150g (5 1/2 oz) mixed red and green grapes, halved

Tools

- large saucepan

- small frying pan

- wooden spoon

- knife

- mixing bowl

This mildly spiced pasta and chicken salad makes a perfect light lunch or is ideal for a school sandwich box.

1 Bring a large pan of lightly salted water to the boil. Add the pasta and cook according to pack instructions. Drain and rinse under cold running water.

2 Meanwhile, in a small frying pan heat the oil, add the curry paste and spring onions and cook for 2 minutes. Leave to cool.

3 Cut away the two sides of the mango, close to the stone. Cut the flesh into criss-cross patterns, press each half inside out and carefully cut off the cubes.

4 Place the spice mixture in a bowl and stir in the lemon juice, yogurt, mayonnaise and coriander. Add the chicken, mango and grapes. Chill until ready to eat.

The spicy and sweet flavours in

Top tip!
If you are a vegetarian, just leave out the chicken. Try adding tofu instead.

this pasta salad are a tasty combination

Potato salad

This simple potato salad substitutes traditional mayonnaise for a lighter creamy sauce, flavoured with chives.

Top tip!
If you like hot and spicy flavours, try adding 15ml (1 tbsp) of horseradish sauce.

Ingredients

- 500g (1lb 2oz) baby new potatoes

- 45ml (3tbsp) reduced fat crème fraîche

- 45ml (3tbsp) low fat yogurt

- 30ml (2tbsp) freshly chopped chives

Tools

- knife

- chopping board

- saucepan

- 2 mixing bowls

- metal spoon

1 Wash and cut any larger potatoes in half.

2 Cook in a pan of lightly salted boiling water for 12 to 15 minutes. Drain and allow to cool. Place in a bowl.

3 In a small bowl, mix together the crème fraîche, yogurt and fresh chives.

4 Gently stir the chive mixture into the potatoes. Season to taste. Keep refrigerated until ready to serve.

This is a healthier version of

Top tip!

Make sure the potatoes are cool, or you will have a warm potato salad!

an old favourite. Perfect for picnics!

Green salad

This salad makes a great accompaniment to grilled fish or chicken. You can add your own favourite vegetables – just remember to keep them green!

Ingredients

- 100g (3½oz) green beans, trimmed and halved

- 100g (3½oz) tenderstem broccoli

- 100g (3½oz) fresh peas

- 150g (5½oz) mixed leaves e.g. baby spinach, rocket and watercress

Dressing:
- 30ml (2tbsp) white wine vinegar

- 30ml (2tbsp) extra virgin olive oil

- 15ml (1tbsp) lemon juice

- 5ml (1tsp) clear honey

- 5ml (1tsp) pesto sauce

Tools

- saucepan

- small mixing bowl

- whisk

- large serving bowl

- jug

1 Add the green beans to a pan of boiling water for 2 minutes. Then add the broccoli and peas and simmer for 3 minutes, and then strain*.

2 Make the dressing. Place all the ingredients in a bowl, season with salt and a little freshly ground black pepper and whisk until combined.

3 Place the salad leaves in a bowl and place the vegetables on top. Drizzle the dressing over the salad and toss together. Serve immediately.

This super-healthy salad is packed

Top tip!

*Once the vegetables are cooked, run them under cold water so they stop cooking and retain their colour.

Veggie spring rolls

These crispy spring rolls filled with vegetables make an easy and delicious snack. Serve with sweet chilli dipping sauce or soy sauce if you prefer.

Ingredients

- 100g (3½oz) beansprouts
- 50g (2oz) cabbage, shredded
- 1 carrot, cut into thin strips
- ½ red pepper, deseeded and thinly sliced
- 6 spring onions, thinly sliced
- 1 clove garlic, crushed
- 2.5cm (1in) piece root ginger, peeled and grated
- 15ml (1tbsp) dark soy sauce
- 6 sheets filo pastry
- 25g (1oz) melted butter

Tools

- mixing bowl
- wooden spoon
- chopping board
- knife
- small bowl
- pastry brush
- baking tray

1 Preheat the oven to 190°C, 375°F, gas mark 5. In a large bowl, mix together all the ingredients, except the filo pastry and butter.

2 Place the sheets of pastry on top of each other and cut in half.

3 Place 1 sheet of the pastry on a board and brush the edges with a little of the melted butter. Place some of the filling on the bottom edge.

Serve these as a starter at a dinner

4 Roll up, folding the ends over. Repeat with remaining pastry and filling.

5 Place on a baking tray and brush with butter. Bake for 12 to 15 minutes until golden. Serve with sweet chilli dipping sauce.

Top tip!
You could try using sweetcorn, peas or mushrooms if you prefer these fillings.

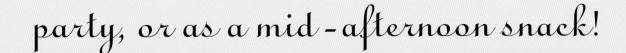

party, or as a mid - afternoon snack!

Baked eggs

You will love these baked eggs, cooked in a rich tomato and pepper sauce. Serve with warmed tortillas or crusty bread for a light lunch or breakfast.

Ingredients

- 15ml (1tbsp) olive oil

- 1 small onion, chopped

- 1 clove garlic, crushed

- 1 mild green chilli, deseeded and finely chopped (optional)

- 1 small green pepper, deseeded and cut into thin strips

- 1 small red pepper, deseeded and cut into thin strips

- 400g (14oz) can chopped tomatoes

- 30ml (2tbsp) tomato ketchup

- 4 eggs

- a little paprika

Tools

- medium saucepan

- wooden spoon

- 2 double, 4 individual or one large ovenproof dish

1 Preheat the oven to 180°C, 350°F, gas mark 4. Heat the oil in a medium pan and add the onion, garlic, chilli and peppers. Cook for 10 to 15 minutes.

2 Stir in the tomatoes and ketchup and season with salt and black pepper. Bring to the boil, then simmer for 5 minutes until thickened.

3 Spoon the mixture into some ovenproof dishes. Make 4 dips and break an egg into each. Place in the oven and bake for 12 to 14 minutes, until just set.

This recipe is based on a traditional

Top tip!

Serve sprinkled with a little paprika, and with warmed floured tortillas.

Mexican recipe called 'huevos rancheros'

Main meals

BBQ chicken skewers

These bite-sized skewers are a tasty option.
Make up double quantities of the sauce and
use half for dipping if you like.

Ingredients

- 12 skinless, boneless chicken thighs

- 1 red and 1 yellow pepper, deseeded and cut into chunks

Barbecue sauce:
- 90ml (6tbsp) tomato ketchup

- 30ml (2tbsp) maple syrup or clear honey

- 30ml (2tbsp) dark soy sauce

- grated rind and juice 1 lime

- 10ml (2tsp) freshly grated ginger

- 30ml (2tbsp) soft brown sugar

Tools

- small saucepan

- wooden spoon

- chopping board

- knife

- mixing bowl

- small wooden skewers (soaked in water for 30 minutes)

- pastry brush

1 Place all the ingredients for the sauce in a small pan, bring to the boil, then simmer for 2 minutes, stirring until the sugar has dissolved. Allow to cool.

2 Cut each chicken thigh into 2 to 3 pieces. Place the cooled sauce in a large bowl.

3 Add the chicken, stir to coat, then leave to marinate for about 30 minutes.

These skewers are ideal served

4 Thread 2 to 3 pieces of chicken onto wooden skewers with pieces of red and yellow pepper. Repeat until all the chicken and peppers have been used up.

5 Line the base of a grill pan with foil, then grill for 10 to 12 minutes, turning occasionally and brushing with the sauce, until the chicken is thoroughly cooked.

Top tip!
Remember to soak the wooden skewers in water for 30 minutes, to prevent them burning.

with rice or a green salad

Cream cheese burgers

These burgers have a surprise cream cheese, herb and garlic filling. Serve in bread rolls with salad or with potato wedges.

These unusual burgers are delicious

Ingredients

Tools

Burgers:
- 675g (1½lb) lean minced beef
- 1 small onion, finely chopped
- 60ml (4tbsp) freshly chopped parsley

Cream cheese filling:
- 75g (3oz) soft cream cheese
- 1 clove garlic, crushed (optional)
- 30ml (2tbsp) freshly chopped chives
- little oil for brushing

- large bowl
- wooden spoon
- small bowl
- pastry brush
- flipper

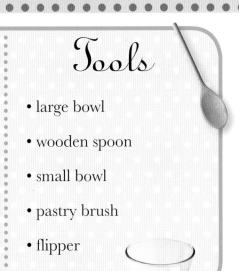

1 In a large bowl, mix together all the ingredients for the burgers, with a little salt and freshly ground black pepper.

2 Divide into 8 equal portions and flatten into rounds.

Top tip!
This recipe works equally well by substituting the beef mince for chicken or turkey mince.

3 In a small bowl, mix together the cream cheese, garlic and chives. Place a quarter of the mixture onto 4 of the burger rounds.

4 Place the other 4 burgers rounds on top and pinch together the edges. Mould into 4 burgers. Chill for 30 minutes.

5 Brush the burgers with a little oil and grill for 8 to 9 minutes each side, until thoroughly cooked through. Serve in bread rolls with salad.

and much tastier than shop - bought ones

Ingredients

- 5ml (1tsp) sunflower oil

- 100g (3½oz) chorizo sausage, skin removed and chopped

- 1 onion, chopped

- 3 skinless chicken breasts, cubed

- 225g (8oz) easy cook long grain rice

- 400g (14oz) can chopped tomatoes

- 450ml (¾pt) hot chicken stock

- 5ml (1tsp) dried mixed herbs

- 1 red and green pepper, deseeded and cubed

- 50g (2oz) frozen peas

- 6 spring onions, chopped

Tools

- large saucepan

- wooden spoon

- heatproof jug

Jambalaya

This lightly spiced Cajun rice dish originated in Louisiana in the USA. The recipe can be easily adapted by adding your favourite vegetables or tofu.

1 Heat the oil in a large pan. Add the chorizo and onion and cook for 2 to 3 minutes, until the paprika oil from the chorizo is released.

2 Add the chicken and cook for 3 to 4 minutes until lightly browned on all sides. Stir in the rice until coated in the oil.

3 Add the tomatoes, stock and herbs. Cover and simmer for 15 minutes, stirring occasionally.

4 Add the peppers, peas and spring onions and cook, covered for a further 10 minutes, until the rice is tender and most of the liquid has been absorbed.

For a spicier taste add 1tsp of hot chilli

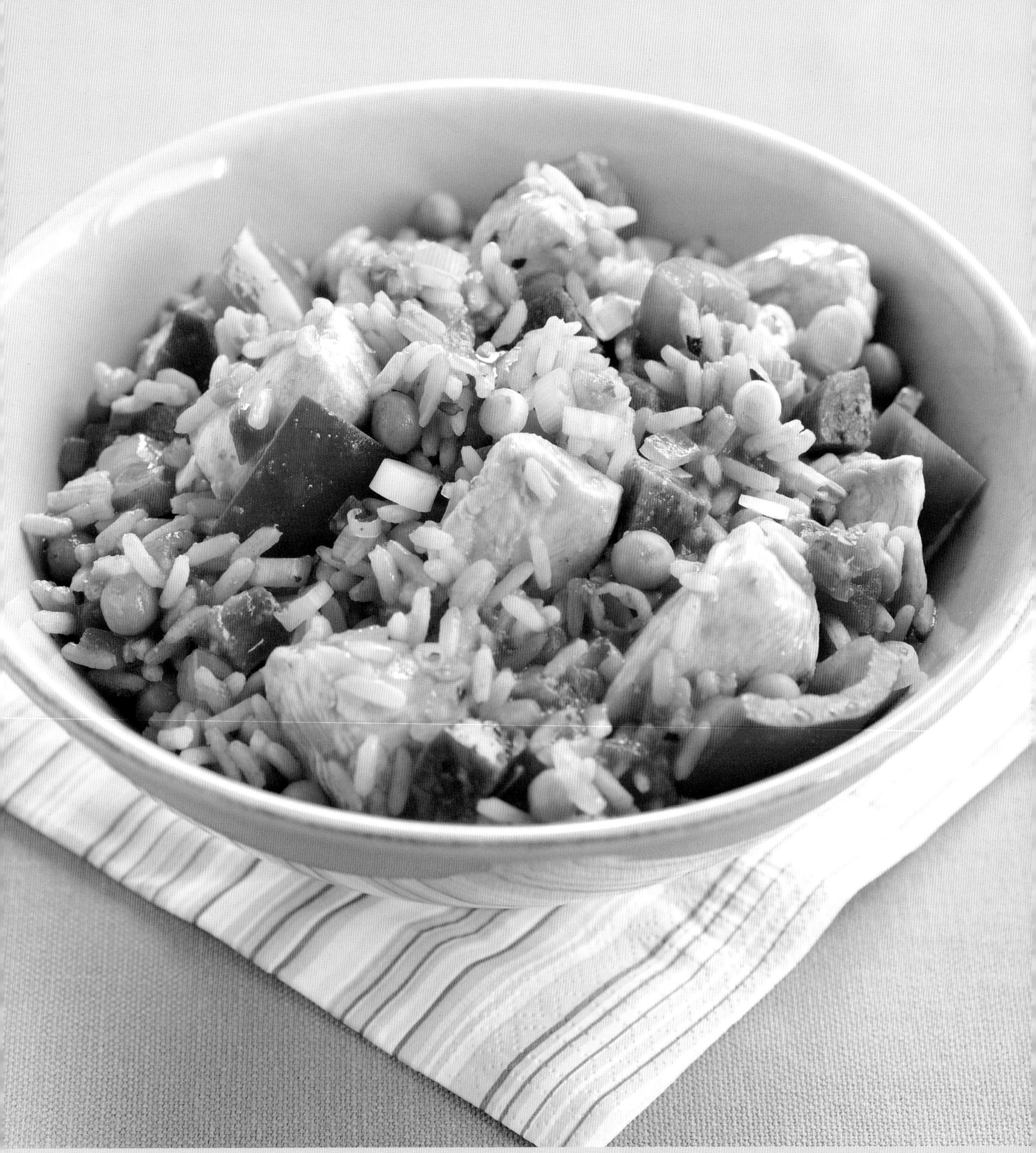

powder or a dash of Tabasco sauce

Mini fish cakes

Serve these bite-sized fish cakes on cocktail sticks to make them easier to dip into the creamy lemon mayonnaise.

Use the discarded potato on page 50

Ingredients

Fish cakes:
- 400g (14oz) fresh salmon fillets
- 400g (14oz) cooked potato (use discarded potato from p50)
- 50g (2oz) frozen peas, defrosted
- 150g (5¹/₂oz) fresh breadcrumbs
- 60ml (4tbsp) freshly

chopped parsley
- 2 eggs, beaten
- sunflower oil for frying

Lemon mayonnaise:
- 250ml (9floz) reduced fat mayonnaise

- grated zest and juice ¹/₂ lemon

Tools

- medium saucepan or frying pan with lid
- 4 mixing bowls
- 3 metal spoons
- plate
- non-stick frying pan
- flipper

1 Place the fish in the pan. Add a little water, and bring to the boil. Cover and cook for 5 to 6 minutes. Allow to cool, then flake, removing any skin and bones.

2 Place the potato, peas and salmon in a bowl. Mix gently until combined and season to taste.

3 Mix the breadcrumbs with the parsley and place on a plate.

4 Place a heaped teaspoon of the salmon mixture in your hands, roll into a ball, then flatten. Dip into the egg, then coat in the breadcrumb mixture.

5 Heat a little oil in a frying pan and shallow fry the fish cakes for 2 to 3 minutes each side until golden.

6 Mix together the mayonnaise with the lemon zest and juice. Transfer to a bowl. Serve the fish cakes warm or cold on cocktail sticks with the dip.

to make these scrumptious fishcakes

Beef chow mein

'Chow mein' means stir-fried noodles in Chinese Mandarin. You can add whatever you like. Try fish, meat, tofu, prawns or vegetables.

To be totally authentic, try using

Ingredients

- 1 clove garlic, crushed

- 2.5cm (1in) piece root ginger, peeled and grated

- 15ml (1tbsp) light soy sauce

- 15ml (1tbsp) rice wine vinegar or sherry

- 350g (12oz) beef steak, (e.g. rump) thinly sliced

- 225g (8oz) dried egg noodles

- 15ml (1tbsp) sunflower oil

- 75g (3oz) mangetout, halved

- 100g (3¹/₂oz) small broccoli florets

- 3 spring onions, sliced

- 1 red pepper, deseeded and thinly sliced

- 100g (3¹/₂oz) beansprouts

- 30ml (2tbsp) oyster sauce

- 10ml (2tsp) toasted sesame oil

Tools

- mixing bowl

- metal spoon

- saucepan

- wooden spoon

- wok/frying pan

1 In a bowl, mix together the garlic, ginger, soy sauce and rice wine vinegar or sherry. Add the sliced beef and stir, then leave to marinate for 10 minutes.

2 Meanwhile, cook the egg noodles. Place in a pan of boiling water and cook for 4 minutes, drain well and return to the pan to keep warm.

3 Heat the sunflower oil in a large wok or frying pan. Add the beef and stir fry for 4 to 5 minutes until browned.

4 Add the mangetout, broccoli, spring onions, and pepper. Stir fry for 2 to 3 minutes.

5 Add the noodles, beansprouts, oyster sauce and sesame oil, then stir fry for a further 2 minutes.

chopsticks to eat this oriental dish

Cheesy potato skins

Crispy bacon and melted cheese make these potato skins a firm favourite. If you and your friends don't like bacon, substitute it with tuna or chicken or leave it out completely.

Ingredients

- 4 large baking potatoes
- oil for brushing
- 8 rashers smoked streaky bacon
- 2.5ml (½tsp) paprika
- 50g (2oz) mature

Cheddar cheese, grated

- 50g (2oz) mozzarella cheese, grated
- 6 spring onions, chopped

Dip:
- 150ml (¼pt) sour cream
- 60ml (4tsp) fresh chives

Tools

- fork
- pastry brush
- baking sheet
- knife
- chopping board
- wooden spoon
- frying pan
- 2 spoons
- small bowl

1 Preheat the oven to 200°C, 400°F, gas mark 6. Prick the potatoes with a fork and brush them with oil. Bake for 1 hour, until cooked. Cool slightly.

2 Cut up the bacon rashers into small pieces. Place the bacon in a frying pan and dry fry, until lightly browned.

3 Cut the potatoes in half and scoop out the flesh with a spoon, leaving a thin layer. Cut each potato in half lengthways to make boat shapes.

These easy-to-make filled potato skins

4 Place on a baking sheet, season and sprinkle over a little paprika. Top with half of the bacon pieces. Mix together the cheeses and spring onions and sprinkle over the potatoes. Top with the remaining bacon.

5 Return the potato skins to the oven until golden. Cool for 10 minutes. Mix together the dip ingredients and serve with the skins.

Top tip!

Make sure the potatoes get really crispy in the oven – it will be worth the wait!

are a delicious option for a party!

Butternut squash soup

This substantial soup is made from roasted butternut squash, but you could try it with pumpkin instead if you prefer.

This wholesome, warming soup

Ingredients

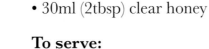

- 1kg (2lb 4oz) butternut squash
- 15ml (1tbsp) vegetable oil
- 1 onion, chopped
- 600ml (1pt) hot vegetable stock
- 30ml (2tbsp) clear honey

To serve:
French stick, Gruyère cheese and freshly chopped parsley

Tools

- knife
- 3 spoons
- chopping board
- vegetable peeler
- baking tray
- measuring jug
- food processor
- saucepan

1 Preheat the oven to 200°C, 400°F, gas mark 6. Cut the butternut squash in half lengthways, then using a spoon scoop out the seeds and pith.

2 Cut into large chunks, then using a peeler, remove the skin. Cut these into 2.5cm (1in) cubes.

3 Place on a baking tray, season with salt and freshly ground black pepper, then drizzle over the oil. Roast for 20 minutes, then remove from the oven.

4 Add the onion and stir. Return to the oven and cook for a further 15 minutes.

5 Place the butternut squash and onion in a food processor with half of the stock and blend until smooth.

6 Place the purée in a saucepan with the remaining stock and honey. Simmer for 3 to 4 minutes. Serve with slices of toasted French stick, Gruyère and parsley.

is perfect for a cold day

Sweet potato lasagne

This lasagne is lighter than a traditional lasagne. Ricotta cheese mixed with fresh basil replaces the traditional béchamel sauce.

Ingredients

- 4 medium tomatoes, quartered

- 1 red onion, cut into 8 wedges

- 3 sweet potatoes, (about 450g (1lb), peeled and thickly sliced

- 2 courgettes, sliced

- 1 red pepper, deseeded and cubed

- 1 yellow pepper, deseeded and cubed

- 15ml (1tbsp) olive oil

- 500g (1lb 2oz) ricotta cheese

- 45ml (3tbsp) freshly chopped basil

- 100g (3½oz) Cheddar cheese, grated

- 100ml (3½floz) double cream

- 1 medium egg, beaten

- 8 sheets fresh lasagne (about 125g (4oz)

Tools

- chopping board

- knife

- 3 mixing bowls

- roasting tin

- metal spoon

- large ovenproof dish

1 Preheat the oven to 180°C, 350°F, gas mark 4. Place all the vegetables in a bowl and add the olive oil. Season with salt and freshly ground black pepper.

2 Place the vegetables in a roasting tin. Cook for 40 minutes, stirring occasionally until tender.

3 Meanwhile in a bowl, combine the ricotta with the cream, basil, half the cheese and the egg.

It might take a while to cut up all the

4 Arrange half the vegetables in the bottom of an ovenproof dish, place half the lasagne sheets over the top, then spoon over half the ricotta mixture.

5 Repeat once more, finishing with a layer of the cheese mixture. Sprinkle over the remaining cheese and bake for 35 to 40 minutes until golden and bubbling.

Top tip!
Use fresh lasagne sheets as there is no sauce for dried sheets to soak up.

Pizza squares

There will certainly be a topping to please everyone in this recipe, which makes 2 large pizzas. Why not top one with meat toppings and one with vegetarian toppings?

Top tip!
Try toppings like peppers, pineapple, ham, pepperoni, red onion, sweetcorn or tomatoes.

These pick and mix pizzas allow you

Ingredients

Dough:
- 2.5ml (½tsp) caster sugar
- 5ml (1tsp) active dried yeast
- 350ml (12floz) lukewarm water
- 5ml (1tsp) salt
- 500g (1lb 2oz) strong white bread flour
- 15ml (1tbsp) olive oil

Tomato sauce:
- 300ml (½pt) passata
- 30ml (2tbsp) tomato purée
- 2.5ml (½tsp) sugar
- 5ml (1tsp) dried mixed herbs
- 200g (7oz) grated mozzarella cheese

Tools

- mixing bowl
- metal spoon
- saucepan
- 2 baking sheets
- sieve
- knife
- damp cloth
- wooden spoon
- rolling pin

1 Put the sugar, yeast and water in a bowl, mix and leave for 5 minutes. In another bowl, sift the flour and salt, then add the oil and the yeast mixture.

2 Stir with a knife to form a dough then knead for 4 to 5 minutes. Place in a bowl, cover with a clean damp cloth and leave in a warm place for 1 hour.

3 Meanwhile, make the tomato sauce. Place all the ingredients in a small pan and simmer gently for 5 minutes, allow to cool.

4 Preheat the oven to 220°C, 450°F, gas mark 7. Using a floured hand, punch the dough to knock out the air, then knead lightly on a floured surface.

5 Divide the dough in half, then roll out each to a rectangle on the baking sheets. Spoon the tomato sauce over, then sprinkle with the cheese.

6 Turn one into a meat pizza and one into a vegetarian pizza. Bake for 15 minutes until golden, before cutting each into squares.

to create your own taste sensation!

Desserts

Blueberry ice cream

This ice cream is so simple to make! Just mix all the prepared ingredients together and freeze.

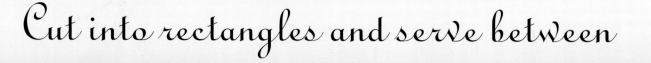

Cut into rectangles and serve between

Ingredients

- 300g (10½oz) fresh blueberries
- 30ml (2tbsp) caster sugar
- grated zest and juice 1 unwaxed lemon
- 300ml (½pt) double cream

- 500g (1lb 2oz) natural bio milk yogurt
- 30ml (2tbsp) icing sugar

Tools

- saucepan
- wooden spoon
- bowl
- 2 spoons
- fine sieve

- large mixing bowl
- electric or hand whisk
- freezerproof container
- fork

1 Place the blueberries in a pan with the caster sugar and lemon zest and juice. Bring to the boil, then simmer for 4 to 5 minutes until the berries burst.

2 Remove from the heat and press through a fine sieve into a bowl, to make a glossy purple coulis. Leave to cool.

Top tip!

Place in the fridge for 15 minutes before serving to soften slightly.

3 Place the cream in a large bowl and with an electric or hand whisk, lightly whip until just starting to thicken.

4 Using a metal spoon, fold in the yogurt and icing sugar until well combined and smooth, then stir in the blueberry coulis.

5 Transfer to a freezerproof container with a lid. Place in freezer for 4 to 5 hours until frozen. Remove every hour and break up the ice crystals with a fork.

wafers for a sophisticated treat!

Very berry jelly

These individual jellies are made using a mixture of frozen berries. Alternatively you could just use one type of berry, such as frozen raspberries or blueberries.

Ingredients

- 135g (5oz) pack of raspberry or blackcurrant flavour jelly
- 150g (5½oz) mixed frozen berries

Tools

- heatproof jug
- spoon
- jelly moulds

1 Place the jelly into a measuring jug and pour over 300ml (½pt) boiling water. Stir until the jelly has dissolved.

2 Stir the fruit into the jug. Top up with cold water to make 600ml (1pt), if necessary.

3 Spoon the mixture between one large jelly mould or four individual moulds and place in the fridge for about 3 hours until set.

Make sure you leave enough time

Top tip!
Using frozen berries prevents them from floating to the top.

to let these yummy jellies set!

Apple crumble sundae

Layers of apple, crunchy crumble, toffee sauce and ice cream are layered up in tall glasses to make a delicious sundae, which is a variation on an old favourite.

Top tip!

Use good quality vanilla ice cream – your sundaes won't be as delicious if you don't!

Serve these sundaes in traditional

Ingredients

Crumble mixture:
- 100g (3½ oz) plain flour
- 50g (2oz) butter, diced
- 50g (2oz) demerara sugar

Apple compote:
- 3 cooking apples, peeled, cored and chopped
- 50g (2oz) caster sugar
- juice ½ lemon
- 90ml (8tbsp) cold fudge sauce (see page 70) or ready made toffee sauce
- 8 scoops vanilla ice cream

Tools

- medium bowl
- baking tray
- baking paper
- medium saucepan
- wooden spoon
- fork

1 Place the flour and butter in a bowl and rub them together with your fingertips until the mixture resembles fine breadcrumbs. Stir in the sugar.

2 Preheat the oven to 200°C, 400°F, gas mark 6. Line a baking tray with baking paper, and pour the mixture on top. Cook for 8 to 10 minutes until golden.

3 Meanwhile, place the apples, sugar and lemon juice in a medium pan. Cover and cook over a gentle heat for 12 to 15 minutes, stirring occasionally.

4 Leave the apple compote to cool with the lid off. Using your fingers or a fork, break up the cooled crumble topping.

5 Layer each sundae glass with apple compote, crumble, ice cream and toffee sauce and serve with long spoons.

Top tip!

Serve warm with ice cream to get a deliciously different dessert!

sundae glasses for a retro feel

Raspberry cheesecake

This fruity cheesecake is so simple to make. The jelly adds flavour and also sets the cheesecake.

Light, creamy and delicious, this

Ingredients

- 75g (3oz) unsalted butter
- 150g (5¹⁄₂oz) digestive biscuits
- 135g (5oz) pack of raspberry flavour jelly
- 200ml (7floz) evaporated milk, chilled
- 200g (7oz) soft cream cheese
- 100g (3¹⁄₂oz) raspberries
- a few raspberries for decoration

Tools

- 20cm (8in) round loose-bottomed sandwich tin
- baking paper
- food bag
- rolling pin
- saucepan
- 3 metal spoons
- heatproof jug
- large bowl
- electric whisk

1 Line the base of a 20cm (8in) round loose-bottomed sandwich tin with baking paper.

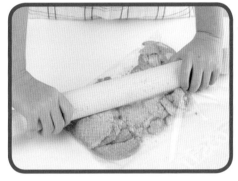

2 Place the biscuits in a food bag and crush with a rolling pin (or you can do this in a food processor).

3 Melt the butter in a saucepan and stir in the crushed biscuits. Press into the tin and chill.

4 Break the jelly into pieces. Then, in a heatproof jug, put the jelly in 100ml (3¹⁄₂floz) boiling water, stir until dissolved.

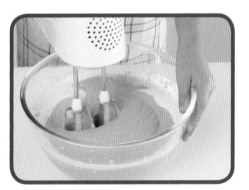

5 In a large bowl, whisk the milk until light and fluffy and doubled in volume. Whisk in the cream cheese, until the mixture is smooth. Whisk in the jelly.

6 Roughly chop the raspberries and stir into the mixture. Pour over the biscuit base and leave to chill for 2 hours. Serve decorated with extra raspberries.

cheesecake is heavenly to eat

Fruit & choc fondue

This dessert is so simple to make. Serve the fruit on cocktail sticks to make dipping easier.

Ingredients

- 250g (9oz) mixed fruit
- 200g (7oz) good quality white chocolate, roughly chopped
- 150ml ($^1/_4$pt) double cream
- 50g (2oz) unsalted butter, diced
- 5ml (1tsp) vanilla extract

Tools

- knife
- bowl
- chopping board
- saucepan
- wooden spoon

1 Prepare the fruit if necessary, remove the stalks from the strawberries and cut the banana into bite-sized pieces. Place on cocktail sticks.

2 Place the chocolate, cream, butter and vanilla extract in a small bowl, set over a pan of simmering water. Heat gently for 5 to 7 minutes, stirring occasionally until the mixture is smooth.

You can use marshmallows instead of fruit

Mango pops

These fruity ice pops are made from pure fruit purée. Decorate with a little melted chocolate and hundreds and thousands.

Ingredients

- 2 large ripe mangoes
- 30ml (2tbsp) icing sugar
- juice 1 lime
- 150g (5½oz) plain or milk chocolate, broken into pieces
- 50g (2oz) hundreds and thousands

Tools

- knife
- chopping board
- food processor
- ice lolly moulds and sticks

1 Copy step 3 on page 28. Place the mango in a food processor with the icing sugar and lime juice and blend to a smooth purée.

2 Pour into 8 moulds and put the sticks in. Freeze for 6 hours. Melt the chocolate and dip the pops in, then dip in the hundreds and thousands. Keep in the freezer until ready to serve.

These fruity pops are a healthy treat

Banana fritters

These bananas are cooked in a light batter, coated with sesame seeds and served with a delicious warm fudge sauce. For extra indulgence add a scoop of vanilla ice cream.

Ingredients

- 4 bananas, peeled and each cut into 4 pieces

- sunflower oil for frying

Fudge sauce:
- 75g (3oz) unsalted butter

- 150g (5¹/₂oz) light soft brown sugar

- 150ml (¹/₄pt) single cream

- 15ml (1tbsp) golden syrup

Batter:
- 125g (4oz) self-raising flour

- 30ml (2tbsp) caster sugar

- 175ml (6floz) milk

- 60ml (4tbsp) sesame seeds

Tools

- large saucepan

- wooden spoon

- large bowl

- large metal spoon

- teaspoon

- slotted spoon

- kitchen paper

1 Place all the fudge sauce ingredients in a pan and cook gently for 2 to 3 minutes. Stirring continuously, bring to the boil for 3 minutes, until thickened.

2 Leave in the pan to cool slightly. Meanwhile, heat a pan ¹/₃ of the volume full of oil, until a piece of bread goes golden brown when dropped in.

3 Mix all the batter ingredients together in a large bowl, reserving 30ml (2tbsp) of the sesame seeds. Add the bananas and turn to coat in the batter.

These banana fritters are a

4 Using a slotted spoon, and holding over the bowl, remove the bananas, then sprinkle with some of the reserved sesame seeds.

5 Fry the banana in batches, in the oil for 3 to 4 minutes until golden brown. Remove and drain on kitchen paper. Serve immediately with the fudge sauce.

Top tip!
Eat these as soon as they are cooked as the batter will become soggy if you leave them.

quick and delicious dessert

Strawberry meringues

These delicious pretty meringues are crisp on the outside and soft in the middle. Fill with lightly whipped cream and sliced strawberries.

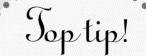

Top tip!
You can make vanilla sugar by leaving a vanilla pod in a jar of sugar.

Unfilled meringues can be kept in an

Ingredients

- 2 large egg whites
- 100g (3½oz) caster sugar
- 150ml (¼pt) double cream
- 15ml (1tbsp) vanilla sugar
- 12 small strawberries, sliced

Tools

- 2 large baking sheets
- baking paper
- large mixing bowl
- electric whisk
- tablespoon
- teaspoon

1 Preheat the oven to 110°C, 225°F, gas mark ¼. Lightly grease 2 large baking sheets and line with baking paper.

2 Place the egg whites into a large, spotlessly clean mixing bowl and whisk them until they form stiff peaks.

3 Add the sugar a tablespoon at a time, whisking well after each addition, until the mixture is smooth, thick and glossy.

4 Place heaped teaspoons of the mixture, spaced a little apart, onto the prepared baking sheets, until you have 30 meringues. Flatten slightly.

5 Bake in a preheated oven for one hour, or until they peel away from the baking paper. Leave to cool. Whisk the vanilla sugar into the cream until thick.

6 Spread some cream on the flat side of a meringue, put some strawberries on top, spread some cream on another meringue and sandwich together.

airtight container for up to 2 days

Baking

Fondant fancies

These gorgeous cakes take a while to prepare
but are well worth the effort.

You can be really creative when

Ingredients

Cake:
- 200g (7oz) unsalted butter or margarine, softened
- 200g (7oz) caster sugar
- grated zest 1 lemon
- 4 medium eggs, beaten
- 200g (7oz) self-raising flour

Filling and icing:
- 75g (3oz) unsalted butter, softened
- 175g (6oz) icing sugar, sifted
- 90 to 120ml (6 to 8tbsp) water
- 15ml (1tbsp) milk
- 15ml (1tbsp) apricot jam
- 100g (3½oz) marzipan
- 1kg (2lb 4oz) fondant icing sugar
- 2 to 3 drops pink food colouring
- writing icing and sugar decorations

Tools

- 2 bowls
- 2 spoons
- 20cm (8in) square tin
- baking paper
- electric whisk
- palette knife
- bread knife
- cling film
- rolling pin
- fork

1 Preheat the oven to 180°C, 350°F, gas mark 4. Grease and line the cake tin. Cream together the butter, sugar and lemon zest.

2 Whisk in the eggs a little at a time, adding a little flour to prevent the mixture curdling. Fold in the rest of the flour. Spoon into the tin and smooth the top.

3 Bake for 20 to 25 minutes. Cool in the tin. Turn out and with a bread knife remove the top layer of the cake, to make it even then cut the cake in half horizontally.

4 Cream together the butter and icing sugar, then add the milk and spread over one half of the cake. Sandwich together. Wrap in cling film and chill for at least 2 hours.

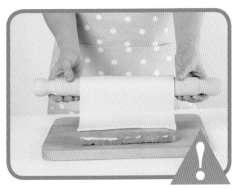

5 Warm the apricot jam and spread over the top. Roll out the marzipan to a 20cm (8in) square and place on top of the cake. Cut the cake into 25 cubes.

6 Mix the fondant icing sugar and water until smooth. Add the pink colouring. Holding over the bowl, drizzle over each cube and decorate as desired. Leave to set.

you come to decorate these cakes!

Caramel shortbread

Caramel shortbread is also known as millionaires' shortbread. It is more like a biscuit than a cake and is definitely for those with a sweet tooth!

Ingredients

Base:
• 50g (2oz) soft brown sugar

• 125g (4oz) butter, softened

• 150g (5½oz) self-raising flour

Caramel topping:
• 397g (14oz) can sweetened condensed milk

• 125g (4oz) butter, diced

• 75g (3oz) soft light brown sugar

• 50ml (2tbsp) golden syrup

Chocolate topping:
• 75g (3oz) white chocolate

• 75g (3oz) plain chocolate

Tools

• 8 x 28cm (7 x 11in) baking tin

• baking paper

• electric whisk

• mixing bowl

• wooden spoon

• saucepan

• 2 bowls

• metal spoon

1 Preheat the oven to 180°C, 350°F, gas mark 4. Grease and line a 18 x 28cm (7 x 11in) tin with baking paper.

2 Cream together the butter and sugar until light and fluffy. Stir in the flour and mix until combined.

3 Press the mixture over the base of the tin and bake for 15 to 20 minutes until golden. Leave to cool.

These shortbread bites are lots of fun

4 Place the caramel topping ingredients in a saucepan. Place over a low heat until dissolved and bring to the boil. Continue to boil, stirring continuously, for 10 to 12 minutes.

5 Pour the caramel topping over the base. Leave to cool completely. Melt the chocolate in separate bowls over a pan of simmering water.

6 Pour the dark and white chocolate over the caramel and swirl together with the back of a spoon. Leave to set, then cut into squares.

to make. What patterns can you create?

Banocolate cookies

These banana-flavoured biscuits are combined with chunks of chocolate. They are best eaten on the day they are made, but can be stored in an airtight container for up to 2 days.

Try using different types of chocolate

Ingredients

- 1 large ripe banana, peeled and sliced

- 100g (3½oz) unsalted butter, cut into pieces

- 1 medium egg, beaten

- 100g (3½oz) soft light brown sugar

- 100g (3½oz) plain flour

- 2.5ml (½tsp) baking powder

- 50g (2oz) whole porridge oats

- 100g (3½oz) plain chocolate, broken into small chunks

Tools

- 2 baking sheets

- knife

- food processor

- mixing bowl

- metal spoon

- cooling rack

1 Preheat the oven to 180°C, 350°F, gas mark 4 and grease 2 baking sheets with butter. Place the banana, butter, sugar and egg in a food processor and blend until smooth.

2 Add the flour, baking powder and oats to the banana mix. Then pulse until combined.

3 Transfer the mixture to a bowl and stir in the chocolate chunks.

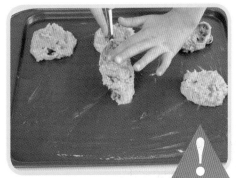

4 Drop heaped dessertspoons of the mixture onto the sheets. Flatten them then bake for 15 to 20 minutes. Cool for 5 minutes, then transfer to a cooling rack.

Top tip!

If you don't like banana, leave it out and add 30ml (2tbsp) of cocoa powder instead.

such as milk, white, dark or flavoured

Gingerbread house

For an extra surprise, fill the centre of the house with more sweets before attaching the roof.

Try making gingerbread men, women

Ingredients

Dough:
- 250g (9oz) unsalted butter, softened
- 150g (5½oz) soft brown sugar
- 2 medium eggs, beaten
- 175ml (6floz) golden syrup
- 30ml (2tbsp) ground ginger
- 625g (1½lb) plain flour
- 10ml (2tsp) bicarbonate of soda

For decoration:
- 1 egg white
- 225g (8oz) icing sugar, sifted
- marshmallows, halved, for the roof and sweets of your choice

Tools

- two 18cm x 10cm (7in x 4in) rectangles for the roof
- two 15cm x 10cm (6in x 4in) rectangles for the sides. Add windows
- two 10cm (4in) squares for the ends, extending 7½cm (3in) from the top edge of the squares to a point. Add a door
- food processor
- cling film
- rolling pin
- baking paper
- knife
- mixing bowl
- spoon
- cooling rack

1 Place the butter and sugar in a food processor and blend until creamy. Add the eggs, golden syrup, ginger, bicarbonate of soda and half the flour and process.

2 Add the remaining flour and process until the mixture forms a ball. Wrap in cling film and chill for 30 minutes. Meanwhile, cut out the templates.

3 Preheat the oven to 180°C, 350°F, gas mark 4. Roll out the dough between 2 pieces of baking paper to 5mm (¼in) thick. Use the templates to cut the dough.

4 Chill for 10 minutes, then bake for 12 minutes. Leave to cool for 2 minutes, then transfer to a cooling rack. Beat the egg white and icing sugar together.

5 Join the front and sides of the house together with a little of the icing and allow to dry. Add the back and roof in the same way. Decorate with icing and sweets.

and children to live in your house

Chocolate cake

This moist cake is simple to make. Decorate
as desired with sweets, chocolate curls
or sprinkles.

This scrummy cake is perfect for

Ingredients

- 200g (7oz) caster sugar

- 200g (7oz) butter, softened

- 4 medium eggs, beaten

- 200g (7oz) self-raising flour. Swap 45ml (3 tbsp) of this for 45ml (3 tbsp) cocoa powder

- 5ml (1tsp) baking powder

- 30ml (2tbsp) milk

Ganache:
- 284ml (10floz) carton double cream

- 30ml (2tbsp) caster sugar

- 200g (7oz) good quality dark chocolate, broken into pieces

Tools

- 2 x 20cm (8in) round sandwich tins

- baking paper

- large mixing bowl

- electric whisk

- spatula

- cooling rack

- saucepan

- wooden spoon

- bowl

- palette knife

1 Preheat oven to 190°C, 375°F, gas mark 5. Butter two 20cm (8in) round sandwich tins and line with non-stick baking paper.

2 In a large bowl, whisk all the cake ingredients together until you have a smooth, soft batter.

3 Divide the mixture between the tins, smooth the surface with a spatula, then bake for about 20 minutes. Turn onto a cooling rack and leave to cool.

4 Place the cream and sugar in a pan and heat until it is about to boil. Put the chocolate in a bowl and pour the cream over. Stir until the chocolate melts.

5 Sandwich the cake together with a little of the ganache. Pour the rest over the top and sides of the cake and smooth with a palette knife. Decorate as desired.

Top tip!
This cake can also be served warm – heat in a microwave and serve with a scoop of ice cream.

birthdays and special occasions

Mini muffins

These bite-sized treats are bursting with fruitiness. You will need to cook them in two batches.

These scrumptious muffins are

Ingredients

- 280g (10oz) plain flour
- 15ml (1tbsp) baking powder
- 2.5ml (½tsp) salt
- 125g (4oz) caster sugar
- 1 large egg
- 2 bananas, roughly chopped
- 240ml (8floz) milk
- 85g (3oz) melted butter
- 200g (7oz) blueberries

Tools

- 2 x 12 mini muffin trays
- sieve
- 2 mixing bowls
- fork
- jug
- metal spoon
- whisk

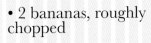

1 Preheat the oven to 200°C, 400°F, gas mark 6. Line 2 x 12 mini muffin trays with paper cases.

2 In a large bowl, sift together flour, baking powder and salt. Stir in the sugar.

3 In a small bowl, mash the bananas with a fork.

4 In a jug, whisk together the egg, milk and butter, then add to the mashed banana, stirring to combine.

5 Add all the wet ingredients to the dry. Stir to just combine, then fold in the blueberries.

6 Spoon into the cases and bake for 10 to 12 minutes or until lightly browned. Refill the muffin tins with paper cases and repeat with the remaining mixture.

a perfect teatime treat!

Cupcakes

Cook these pretty cakes and decorate with pastel colour icings, sweets or crystallised flowers. Stack in a tower as an alternative way to celebrate a birthday party or naming day.

Top tip!

These cakes can be made the day before and stored in an airtight container.

These cakes are easy and quick to

Ingredients

Cakes:
• 150g (5¹⁄₂oz) unsalted butter, softened

• 150g (5¹⁄₂oz) caster sugar

• 150g (5¹⁄₂oz) self-raising flour

• 3 medium eggs, whisked

• 2.5ml (¹⁄₂tsp) vanilla extract

Icing and decoration:
• 225g (8oz) icing sugar, sifted

• 30 to 45ml (2 to 3tbsp) hot water

• 3 different food colourings

• Edible crystallised flowers, sugar strands, hundreds and thousands or sweets

Tools

• 2 x12 bun tins

• 20 paper cases

• 2 mixing bowls

• wooden spoon

• 2 metal spoons

• cooling rack

• knife

• 3 small mixing bowls

1 Line 2 x 12 bun tins with 20 paper cases. Preheat the oven to 180°C, 350°F, gas mark 4.

2 Place the butter, sugar, self-raising flour, eggs and vanilla extract in a bowl and beat with a wooden spoon until pale and creamy

3 Divide between the paper cases. Bake for 15 minutes until golden and just firm. Cool in the tin for 5 minutes, then transfer to a cooling rack to cool.

4 Trim any pointed tops to make a flat surface.

5 Place the icing in a large bowl, gradually beat in sufficient water to give a smooth thick icing, which coats the back of a spoon.

6 Transfer the icing mixture to 3 individual bowls and add a few drops of food colouring to each. Spoon onto the cakes and top with decorations. Allow to set.

make, and even quicker to eat!

89

Chocolate & raspberry brownies

These delicious pretty brownies, dotted with fresh raspberries and white chocolate, are so easy to make.

These yummy white chocolate and raspberry

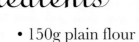

Ingredients

- 250g (9oz) good quality white chocolate
- 75g (3oz) butter
- 125g (4oz) caster sugar
- 2 large eggs beaten
- 5ml (1tsp) vanilla extract
- 150g plain flour
- 2.5ml (½tsp) salt
- 150g (5½oz) fresh raspberries

Tools

- 20cm (8in) square cake tin
- baking paper
- 2 medium bowls
- saucepan
- electric whisk
- sieve
- metal spoon
- plastic spatula
- knife

1 Preheat the oven to 180°C, 350°F, gas mark 4. Grease and line the bottom of a 20cm (8in) square cake tin with baking paper.

2 Break up the chocolate, and put 175g (6oz) in a bowl and set over a pan of simmering water until melted and smooth. Cool slightly.

3 Whisk the butter and sugar together until fluffy in a medium bowl. Whisk in the eggs and vanilla extract, then stir in the melted chocolate.

4 Sift the flour and salt over the mixture and fold in. Then gently fold in the saved broken chocolate and the raspberries.

5 Spoon the mixture into the tin, spread into the corners and level with a plastic spatula. Cook for 30 to 35 minutes. Cool before cutting into squares.

Top tip!

Brownies should be firm on the outside but gooey and fudge-like on the inside.

brownies are a perfect snack!

Drinks

Milkshake

Make your own delicious milkshakes with fresh fruit. This simple drink is healthy and full of natural goodness.

Ingredients

• 400g (14oz) fresh strawberries or 4 bananas

• 600ml (1pt) cold milk

• 8 scoops vanilla ice cream

Tools

• knife

• chopping board

• blender

1 Remove the stalks from the strawberries/peel and chop the banana. Place in a liquidiser or blender and blitz to a purée.

2 Add the milk and ice cream and blend for 1 minute until frothy. Pour into 4 tall glasses and serve. For the banana one, try adding 4tbsp of toffee sauce or try chocolate ice cream instead of vanilla.

Decorate your glass with extra fruit

Hot chocolate

This simple recipe uses good quality chocolate instead of drinking chocolate – the taste is so much better!

Ingredients

- 100g (3½oz) good quality plain, milk or white chocolate

- 600ml (1pt) milk

- few drops of mint, orange or vanilla extract

- 12 marshmallows

- cocoa powder, for dusting

Tools

- grater

- whisk

- saucepan

1 Coarsely grate the chocolate. Place the milk and chocolate in a saucepan and whisk over a moderate heat for 3 to 4 minutes until the chocolate has dissolved.

2 Add a few drops of flavouring. Pour the hot chocolate into 4 mugs and top each with 3 marshmallows. Dust with the cocoa powder.

Deliciously flavoured hot chocolate!

Cherry cordial

Make this cordial when cherries are in season.
Top with chilled sparkling water and
ice for a refreshing drink.

This cherry cordial is a refreshing

Ingredients

- 1kg (2lb 2oz) fresh red cherries
- 600ml (1pt) cold water
- 350g (12oz) caster sugar
- chilled still or sparkling water and ice, to serve

Tools

- knife
- chopping board
- 2 large saucepans
- wooden spoon
- food processor
- sieve
- metal spoon
- sterile jars

1 Cut each cherry in half and remove the stone. Place the stoned cherries in a medium pan with the cold water.

2 Bring to the boil and simmer over a gentle heat for about 15 minutes until the fruit has softened.

3 Leave to cool for 10 minutes, then place in a food processor and blend. (You may need to do this in batches.)

4 Strain through a sieve into a clean pan, pressing the pulp left in the sieve. Add the sugar and, over a low heat, stir until dissolved.

5 Simmer for 5 minutes. Pour into sterilised jars and store in a cool place. Pour a little of the cordial into a glass and top with chilled water and ice.

Top tip!

To make a blackcurrant cordial replace the cherries with the same weight of blackcurrants.

drink for a hot summer's day!

Watermelon punch

This pretty red punch is made from
watermelon and raspberries.

Ingredients

- 1 small watermelon
- 300g (10¹/₂oz) fresh raspberries
- 1 orange, sliced
- 20 fresh mint leaves
- 20 ice cubes
- extra raspberries, to serve

Tools

- knife
- chopping board
- blender
- large bowl
- sieve

1 Cut the watermelon in half, then cut into wedges and remove the skin. Cut the flesh into chunks – you need about 1kg (2lb 2oz). Place in a blender with the raspberries and blend until liquified.

2 Strain the mixture through a sieve over a bowl. Pour into a jug or punch bowl and add the orange slices, mint and ice cubes. Add the extra raspberries. Serve immediately.

This delicious drink is full of goodness

Smoothies

Fruit smoothies not only make a nutritional drink, but can also be served as a healthy snack, or with cereal or toast for breakfast.

Ingredients

• 350g (12oz) mixed berries

• 1 ripe banana

• 500g (1lb 2oz) low fat or fat free vanilla bio live yogurt

• 300ml ($^1/_2$pt) semi-skimmed milk

Tools

• knife

• blender

1 Peel the banana and roughly break into small pieces. Place in a blender with the berries, yogurt and milk. Whizz until the mixture is thick and smooth.

2 Pour into glasses and serve at once. For a banana and mango smoothie, substitute the berries for 1 large ripe mango and add another banana.

Choose which flavour you like best!

Pink lemonade

There is nothing more refreshing than a cool glass of homemade lemonade. Pink lemonade was traditionally dyed with a little beetroot juice, but this recipe uses cranberry juice for flavour and colour.

Ingredients

- 4 unwaxed lemons
- 100g (3½oz) caster sugar
- 600ml (1pt) boiling water
- 200ml (7floz) cranberry juice, chilled
- 200ml (7floz) water, chilled
- ice and lemon slices, to serve

Tools

- potato peeler
- knife
- chopping board
- wooden spoon
- heatproof jug
- mini-sieve
- serving jug

1 Using a potato peeler, peel the zest from the lemons, leaving as much of the white pith on the lemons as possible. Squeeze the juice from the lemons.

2 Pour the lemon juice into a large heatproof jug, add the sugar and lemon zest. Pour over the boiling water and stir until the sugar has dissolved.

3 Leave to cool. Then strain the lemonade into a serving jug.

4 Stir in the cranberry juice and chilled water. Sweeten with extra sugar if desired and serve in glasses with ice and a slice of lemon.

This decorative drink is

very pretty and tastes great!

Sweets & treats

Marshmallow squares

These delicious squares of marshmallow and toasted rice are so easy to make and will keep in an airtight container for up to a week.

Ingredients

- 250g (9oz) marshmallows
- 2.5ml (½tsp) vanilla extract
- 100g (3½oz) butter, diced
- 175g (6oz) toasted rice cereal

Tools

- 18 x 28cm (7 x 11in) oblong tin
- saucepan
- wooden spoon
- metal spoon
- knife

1 Grease a 18 x 28cm (7x11in) oblong tin. Place 200g (7oz) of the marshmallows, with the butter and vanilla extract in a medium saucepan.

2 Place over a medium heat and cook until the butter and marshmallows have melted. Roughly chop the remaining marshmallows.

3 Mix the toasted rice with the marshmallow mixture, then stir in the extra marshmallows. Spoon the mixture into the tray and press down with the back of a spoon.

4 Allow to cool in the tray and then cut into squares.

These are perfect to make if you don't have

Top tip!
Use different coloured
marshmallows to
make your squares
look more
colourful.

much time as they are so quick & easy!

Toffee popcorn

Homemade popcorn is great fun to make and tastes much better than shop-bought.

Ingredients

- 30ml (2tbsp) corn oil
- 100g (3$^{1}/_{2}$oz) popping corn
- 50g (2oz) butter
- 50g (2oz) soft brown sugar
- 75ml (3tbsp) golden syrup

Tools

- 2 medium saucepans
- large mixing bowl
- spoon

1 Heat the oil in a saucepan. Add the corn and, with the lid on, shake to coat in the oil. Over a medium heat, shake the pan occasionally until the corn has popped.

2 Remove from the heat. Place the butter, sugar and syrup in another pan. Stir together over a medium heat until the butter has melted and the sugar has dissolved.

3 Put the popcorn into a large mixing bowl and drizzle the toffee sauce over the top.

4 Stir until the popcorn is coated. Stop stirring when the sauce has cooled and is setting. Leave until cool enough to eat.

This recipe makes the perfect

Top tip!

Wait until there are 3 to 5 seconds between each 'pop' before you turn off the heat.

accompaniment to your favourite movies!

Peppermint creams

These sophisticated sweets make a gorgeous
gift for a friend – or maybe for yourself!

Ingredients

- 450g (1lb) icing sugar, sifted

- 120 to 135ml (8 to 9tbsp) sweetened condensed milk

- few drops peppermint extract or essence

- few drops green food colouring

- 150g (5½oz) plain chocolate

Tools

- mixing bowl

- metal spoon

- rolling pin

- small circular cookie cutter

- baking paper

- heatproof bowl

- saucepan

1 Place the icing sugar in a large bowl and add the condensed milk. Stir until you have a crumbly mixture.

2 Add a few drops of the peppermint extract or essence, and a few drops of green food colouring. Knead until you have a smooth firm mixture.

3 Lightly dust the work surface with a little icing sugar and roll out to 5mm (½in) thick. Cut into rounds with a small cutter. Leave to dry on a piece of baking paper.

4 Melt the chocolate in a heatproof bowl over a pan of simmering water, then dip each cream into the melted chocolate. Leave to set.

The combination of chocolate

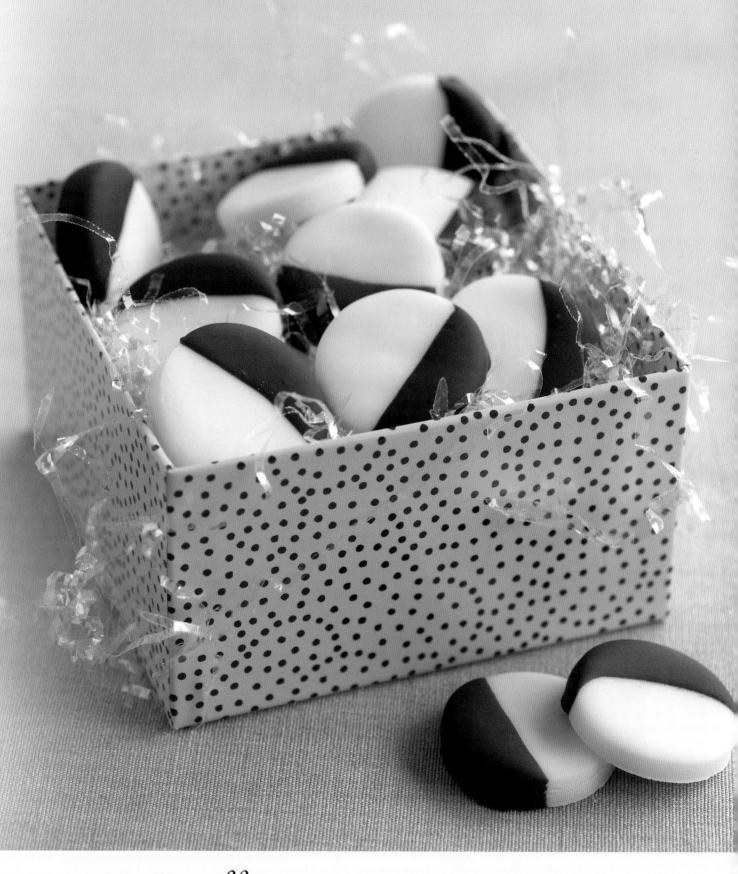

and mint flavours is scrumptious!

Ultimate fudge

Homemade sweets make wonderful gifts or treats. This basic recipe can be adapted to make chocolate or raisin fudge.

Top tip!
Like all sweets and treats, eat fudge in moderation or you will feel ill!

Ingredients

- 450g (1lb) caster sugar
- 50g (2oz) unsalted butter, diced
- 170g (6floz) can evaporated milk
- 150ml (¼pt) milk
- 2.5ml (½tsp) vanilla extract

Tools

- 18cm (7in) shallow non-stick square tin
- medium heavy-based saucepan
- sugar thermometer
- wooden spoon
- knife

1 Grease an 18cm (7in) shallow non-stick square tin.

 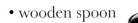

2 Gently heat the sugar, butter and milks in a saucepan, stirring with a wooden spoon until all the sugar has dissolved.

3 Bring to the boil and simmer gently, stirring continuously, for about 20 to 25 minutes.

Give fudge as a gift, beautifully

4 A sugar thermometer should reach a temperature of 116°C (240°F). Remove from the heat, add the vanilla extract.

5 Beat until the mixture is thick and paler in colour. Pour into the prepared tin and leave to cool. When cold, cut into squares.

Top tip!
For chocolate fudge stir in 150g (5¹/₂oz) melted plain chocolate in place of the vanilla. For raisin fudge, stir in 75g (3oz) chopped raisins.

presented in a homemade giftbox (p117)

Chocolate truffles

You can flavour these truffles with vanilla, orange or peppermint extract and roll them in cocoa powder, chocolate sprinkles or chopped nuts.

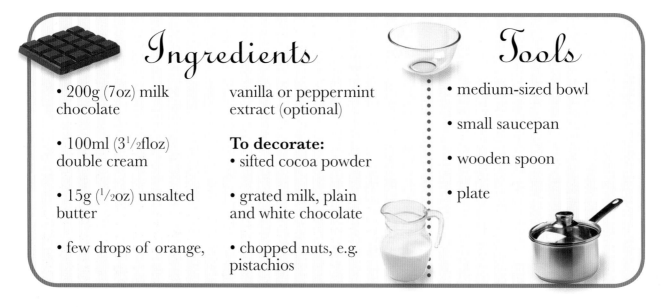

Ingredients

- 200g (7oz) milk chocolate
- 100ml (3½floz) double cream
- 15g (½oz) unsalted butter
- few drops of orange,
- vanilla or peppermint extract (optional)

To decorate:
- sifted cocoa powder
- grated milk, plain and white chocolate
- chopped nuts, e.g. pistachios

Tools

- medium-sized bowl
- small saucepan
- wooden spoon
- plate

1 Break the chocolate into small pieces in a medium sized bowl. Put the cream in a small saucepan with the butter and bring slowly to the boil.

2 Immediately pour over the broken chocolate. With a wooden spoon, stir until the mixture is smooth and all the chocolate has melted.

3 Stir in a few drops of orange or peppermint extract if using. Cover and allow the mixture to cool for about 30 minutes at room temperature.

For a pure and simple hit of chocolate,

4 Chill in the refrigerator for about 2 hours. Using a teaspoon, scoop out bite-sized pieces. Dust your hand lightly with cocoa powder and roll into balls.

5 Immediately roll the truffles in sifted cocoa powder, grated chocolate or nuts. Place in individual foil sweet cases and chill. They will keep for up to 10 days.

Top tip!
Alternatively, you can dip the truffles in melted milk, dark or white chocolate.

these truffles are just the thing!

Coconut ice

This coconut ice recipe requires no cooking – just mix all the ingredients together and leave to set.

Try using different food colourings

Ingredients

- 397g (14oz) can sweetened condensed milk
- 500g (1lb 2oz) icing sugar, sifted
- 350g (12oz) desiccated coconut
- few drops pink food colouring

Tools

- 20cm (8in) square cake tin
- baking paper
- mixing bowl
- metal spoon

1 Line a 20cm (8in) square cake tin with baking paper.

2 In a large bowl, combine the condensed milk with the icing sugar, then stir in the coconut, to form a stiff mixture.

Top tip!

If stored in an airtight container, the coconut ice will keep for up to 3 weeks.

3 Divide the mixture in half and using your hands, press half into the tin.

4 Knead the remaining mixture with a few drops of pink colouring and dusted with a little icing sugar.

5 Press this over the white layer. Refrigerate until set, then cut into squares.

instead of the traditional pink and white

Crafts

Gift boxes

Make these beautiful gift boxes filled
with scrumptious
sweets to give as
gifts to friends
or family.

You will need

- plain box
- paint
- paintbrush
- scissors
- a selection of coloured paper
- double-sided tape
- glue
- ribbons
- glitter and gems
- tissue paper

1 Paint the box, then cut out
some flower shapes from the
different papers and stick to
the lid of the box.

2 Add some ribbon around
the box and decorate with
glitter and gems. Line with
tissue paper.

Gifts that friends and family will treasure

Invitations

Making your own party invitations will give your party a sense of occasion. Your friends will appreciate the extra effort you have put in to make your party a special event!

Be sure to add lots of glitter and sparkle

You will need

- 1 sheet of white A4 card
- 1 sheet of pink A5 card
- ruler
- pencil
- scissors
- various sheets of coloured card and glitter paper
- adhesive gems, sequins and felt flowers
- glue
- ribbons

1 Fold the piece of white card in half to make the base. Draw a border of 2.5cm (1in) around the pink card and then cut out the middle.

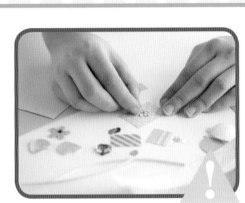

2 Cut some balloon and present shapes out of different coloured card. Accessorise with glitter paper to look like ribbon and sparkly jewels.

Top tip!
Deliver your invitations to your friends and have a great time at your party!

3 Cut out a dress shape using card. Use glitter paper for the coathanger. Stick strips of fabric in a concertina to some double sided tape for the ruffles.

4 Using gems, ribbon and felt flowers, accessorise the border. Stick the border on to the white card. Stick the presents, balloons and dress inside the border.

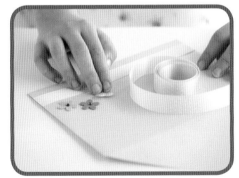

5 Accessorise the envelope with ribbon, felt flowers and gems. Remember to write the details of your party inside!

to make these cards truly extraordinary!

Place settings

If you are planning a dinner party, why not make these gorgeous named place settings to show your guests where to sit.

Lisa

If your dinner party has a theme you

You will need

- 2 different coloured pieces of card
- pencil
- ruler
- scissors

- double-sided tape or craft glue
- cotton
- needle
- sticky tape

- gems and glitter beads
- glitter glue
- silver star decorations

1 Cut out a thick strip of card and divide into 3 equal sections, with a 1cm (½in) strip at one end. Score along all the lines.

2 Draw and cut out a pretty shape in the first section.

3 Cover the back of your strip with coloured card so it's not white when you look through your shape.

4 Cut a heart shape out of card. Stick some cotton thread to the heart and thread some beads on using the needle.

5 Attach the cotton thread onto the back of the section with the pretty shape cut out with some sticky tape. Trim the end of the cotton thread neatly.

6 Using double sided sticky tape or glue, stick the 1cm (½in) strip to the back of the front section.

can adapt these place settings to match

Drink mixers

These pretty mixers will add a touch of class to any beverage. Wash them carefully after use and use again and again.

Match the colour of the drink mixers

You will need

- selection of straws
- selection of papers, material and card
- sequins and gems
- glue
- double-sided tape

Top tip!
If you don't like these shapes, try making a mixer in the shape of your favourite animal.

Star mixer

1 Cut out two star shapes and stick them on to the top of a straw.

2 Cut smaller star shapes out of different patterned material and card and stick them on top to create a layered effect. Add star sequins to finish.

Flower mixer

1 Cut a pretty flower shape out of card.

2 Cut out some smaller, different flower shapes to stick on top. Make them different shapes. Add gems and stick to the straw.

Butterfly mixer

1 Cut out two butterfly shapes and bend the wings outwards. Cut some pretty shapes out of different coloured card and stick to the wings and body.

2 Stick the butterflies bodies to the top of the straw and decorate the edges of the wings with gems.

to your friends' favourite colours

Folded napkins

These folded napkins are very easy and quick to make. Adding sequins, gems and decorations will add some sparkle to a dinner party. Try experimenting with your favourite colours.

You will need

- lots of coloured paper napkins

- glitter and gems

- craft glue

Top tip!

For an extra special effect, colour-co-ordinate these napkins with the place settings.

1 Place 2 different coloured napkins together and fold them in half and then in half again.

2 Take the top loose corner of the first sheet and fold underneath to make a pocket.

3 Repeat with the other layers, leaving a 1cm (½in) strip between each fold.

These napkins will add an elegant

4 Turn the napkins over and fold the 2 side corners into the centre to create a cone shape.

5 Decorate with gems and sparkles. Open the pocket to place your knife and fork inside.

finishing touch to your table

Glossary

If you don't know what a word means, look it up here!

A

accompaniment a food dish that is served with the main dish. It is often made from vegetables or potato.

B

batch a quantity of things cooked together at the same time.

batter a mixture of flour, egg, and milk or water, used for coating food for frying.

beat to stir or mix an ingredient quickly, to add air.

béchamel a white sauce made from butter, milk and flour.

blend to mix ingredients by hand or in a blender or food processor to form a liquid or smooth mixture.

brown to cook food, usually by baking, frying or grilling, so that it becomes light brown.

C

Cajun descendants of French Canadians.

caramelise to turn brown and sticky when heated. This happens if the food has a sweet coating or sauce.

compote fruit cooked in a syrup.

consistency how thick or thin something is.

cordial a concentrated, sweetened fruit drink.

couscous a North African dish or crushed or coarsely ground wheat.

cream to beat butter and sugar together to add air.

crudités thin strips of raw vegetables, usually served with a dip.

crystallise to form crystals.

curdle when the liquid and solid parts of an ingredient or mixture separate. Milk curdles when over-heated and cakes can curdle if the eggs are too cold or added too quickly.

D

deseed to take the seeds out.

dice to cut food into small cubes.

dissolve to melt a solid into a liquid, usually with heat.

dough a firm mixture of flour, liquid and usually other ingredients, that can be kneaded.

drizzle to pour slowly, in a trickle.

EF

extract a concentrated essence (flavour) of a plant.

filo pastry a flaky pastry made with thin sheets of dough.

fondue a dish in which small pieces of food are dipped in a large pot of sauce.

freezerproof made to withstand being frozen, without cracking or breaking.

GH

ganache an icing or filling made from chocolate and heavy cream.

grate to use a grater to make thin shreds of a food.

grease to spread a thin layer of butter or oil to stop food from sticking to the pan or tin.

griddle to cook food over heat on a special ridged pan that makes black lines.

guacamole a Mexican dip made from avocadoes.

heatproof made to withstand heat without cracking or breaking.

IJK

ingredients the different foods which are added together to make a dish.

knead to fold and press dough with your hands to make it smooth and stretchy.

LM

liquify to blend or process a food until it is liquid.

marinate to soak food in a sauce to add flavour.

mash to crush food like bananas or boiled potatoes to make a smooth mixture.

mix to put ingredients together and stir them.

moderate average, or in the middle.

NOP

non-stick coated with a substance that prevents food from sticking.

nutrition things in food that nourish the body.

ovenproof made to withstand the heat of an oven without cracking or breaking.

pesto an Italian sauce made from pine nuts, cheese and herbs.

pith the white layer underneath the skin of a citrus fruit.

pulp the soft matter left over when water is squeezed from fruit or vegetables.

purée to blend or liquidise food.

QRS

quantity how much of something there is.

season to add salt and pepper to enhance flavour.

salsa a spicy Mexican relish of chopped mixed vegetables, usually with tomatoes, onions and chillies.

shallow fry to fry in about 1 cm ($^1/_2$in) of oil, so that the outside turns golden and crispy.

sift to shake food through a sieve to remove lumps.

simmer to bubble gently below or just at boiling point.

starter a smaller dish, served as a first course before the main course.

stir fry to fry food in a little oil over a high heat, stirring constantly.

sterilise to destroy bacteria and germs, usually with boiling water.

stock a flavoured liquid in which meat, fish or vegetables are cooked.

strain to use a sieve to drain a liquid.

sundae a dish of ice cream served with a topping usually made of fruit, nuts and syrup.

TUV

tofu a soft cheeselike food prepared from soya-bean milk.

vegetarian someone who doesn't eat meat.

volume how much of something there is.

WXYZ

wok a large bowl-shaped pan, used for stir-frying.

whip/whisk to beat into a froth using a whisk or fork, to add air.

zest the outer peel of a citrus fruit, used as a flavouring.

Index